Archaeology
for the
Woman's Soul

Awaken Woman...
Unearth Yourself...
Worship Your Truth...

Corina Luna Dea

Archaeology for the Woman's Soul-
Awaken Woman, Unearth Yourself, Worship Your Truth
Published by Archaeology for the Soul Press
www.archaeologyforthesoul.com
Printed in the United States of America
First edition printing in 2018

Poetry/Transformation/Inspiration/Motivation/Personal Growth/

Design by Yeliz Karagozlu, Tim Jonas and Angela Denby
Cover art by Flora Aube www.floraaube.com
Library of Congress Control Number: 2017952679
ISBN: 978-0-692-19863-6

I dedicate
this book to all the
women before me who sacrificed
themselves in honoring their truth...

You have given me your
strength and courage

And to my parents whom I love
more than I thought...

What Others Are Saying About
"Archaeology for the Woman's Soul"

"Corina Luna Dea reaches deeply into your soul to shed light on eroded memories, to carve out the blockages that have held deeply rooted pain, shame and self-doubt captive. Speaking deeply of her own pain, Corina's journey is our journey. It's the journey of all women stripped from the magnificence of our feminine divinity and left to suffer through life in a patriarchal and, in many cases, misogynistic prison as the invisible nurturer.

Creatively weaving a tapestry of healing and empowering 'take-action' messages, "Archaeology for the Woman's Soul" is a collective opportunity to connect to our own personal stories, pushing us deeper within to touch and tend to the wounds that have never healed. This is not simply a poem, it is the story of becoming one with our pain as we journey into higher awareness and celebrate pain's gift of lessons and guidance.

Corina's encouraging and powerful insight lifts our Spirit into a celebratory stance, empowering our hearts to step into our awakening without fear. She lovingly pushes us to unearth our inner Goddess, worship our truth and unleash our voices to fully live the miracle of being a woman."

- Dr. Rev. Diva Verdun
Personal & Empowerment Guru

I

"It is an honor and a privilege to write this review for Corina. She writes from the heart and in so doing touches the hearts of those who read her work. She demonstrates a wonderful ability to express herself through her own experiences, some very difficult, and portray events in her life in such a way that respects and acknowledges the hurts endured whilst giving voice to the lessons learned. In this way Corina speaks to women from across the globe, regardless of culture, religion or country.

She speaks to women acknowledging often the horrific suffering, struggles and atrocities that women, the world over, face whilst delivering words of understanding, compassion and empowerment. Corina speaks to my heart. I am able to ascertain from the depth and quality of her expression that she "knows." Her writing has uplifted me and I look forward to this writing being available for many more women across the world."

- Cathryn Williams-Ohlson
Community Organizer New Zealand

"Corina... Wow. Your gift of poetic writing and expression is almost more than my soul can take in. You are a gifted writer and conveyor of truth and wisdom. Profound, exquisite, a masterpiece of the soul expressing what so many could not put into words. Simply magnificent. I am truly in awe. Thank you for bestowing the honor of reading this extraordinary song of the woman's heart. Wow."

- Lisa Turley Walker
International Speaker, Writer, Coach

"Corina's poem of love offers an invitation to dig deep and release all of the pain, all of the memories of our feelings of unworthiness. Corina found her inspiration from her sacred connection with Mother Earth. In baring her soul, she has found her solace and her salvation. I was moved to silence, and felt a rush of unhealed emotions upon reading of her journey within. A remembrance of the Divine Feminine, this book is a gift from the heart, an invitation to ignite our own sacred fire and joyfully embrace life!

This book will find its way into your very being surrounding you with the gentle encouragement to unearth what was lost. It is a reminder that we are whole and worthy of all the love and support of the universe. This eloquent poem is a love story like none other. It is an inspirational account of transmuting the darkest crevices of the soul. I invite you to embrace her story - for it is our collective story."

- Sandra Strait
Inspirational Author

"I feel deeply seen and validated reading Corina's words. Over the last year I've explored parts of myself that have been both terrifying and exhilarating, and at times I felt inadequate or wrong or just broken. Corina's words demonstrate how universal our experiences are when we're radically honest about them. Thank you so much for doing your own Soul and Heartwork, Corina. Keep on Woman! I love you."

- Naima Singletary
Community Builder for Soul Workers

"A tender telling of the love affair with self. 'Archaeology for the Woman's Soul' *by Corina Luna Dea. "Woman unearthed. Broken open from ancient agonies, dancing in deep dungeons, excavating tarnished truths. She unmasks and disrobes, falling in love with her shining self. Claiming her soul... captured by rapture, she finds her way home".*

- Bobbie Stuart
Visionary artist, intuitive spiritual
teacher at "Awakening Possibilities."

"As we recover ourselves from a history plagued with patriarchy and deception that has distorted how we see ourselves and others, Corina's poetry offers us the opportunity to find ourselves again and stand in our power as stewards and guardians of this great Earth. Her inspiring words take us on a journey, a most magnificent journey that will awaken the parts of ourselves that may be aching to come to the surface. As her story is every woman's story, the very words that are spoken will begin to transform you in a way that is deeply inspiring, liberating and exciting.

With passion and compassion, Corina's "Archaeology for the Woman's Soul" makes us aware of our sacred qualities and deep inner beauty that is filled with purpose and power to heal and unify, directly impacting all aspects of our lives. Here, we are being called to embark on our own unique path and this book is an incredible guide and companion to open one up to the treasures we were born with, helping us expand the way we see ourselves for what we truly are, in a most potent and profound way. This book helps us to finally come home again."

- Laura Magdalene Eisenhower
Spiritual Guide "Awake in the Dream"
Radio Hostess

Acknowledgements

This book would have never been written without the guided inspiration from my special friend Chantal Christine Boudreau. You have opened me up to believe in myself and what I am here to do. Your vision and belief in my message for humanity gave me the confidence I needed to complete this book.I want to acknowledge my editor, Louisa Dyer for your careful reading of the poem. It made all the difference. You are not only a talented editor, but your higher understanding of the spiritual world helped me clarify the message of the poem. I am truly grateful for all your help.

From the deepest place in my heart I want to mention my Facebook friends Sherri Lynn Dunn, Sandra Strait, Margaret Minkus Dubay, Amma Sophia, Karen Shell Bratton, Lisa Turley Walker, Bernedette Giorgi, Deborah Harlow and so many others. Thank you for your support and encouragement throughout the long five years from the time the poem was written until it was published in this form.

Many thanks to the graphic designers Yeliz Karagozlu and Tim Jonas for their dedicated work. And to Angela Denby who put the final touches on the book cover. (www.angeladenby.com) And last, but not least, I am deeply grateful to the talented California Artist Flora Aube for the beautiful painting, titled "Hope" that covers my book. Flora's artwork can be found at www.floraaube.com.

Foreword

Are you willing to be inspired? To feel empowered? If so, you are holding a book that will wake you up not only to your power, but to the incredible beauty of Divine Spirit flowing through your life. As an avid reader, it is seldom I come across something that feeds my soul as well as my mind, that nourishes my spirit while also teaching me practical tools for living well.

Every woman, and every man who knows a woman, will benefit from reading this incredible odyssey from Romania to the United States, from Communism to Freedom, from the self-loathing of victimhood to the glory of self-empowerment. And then Corina tells you how you can do it as well!

"Archaeology for the Woman's Soul" plumbs the depths and climbs the heights of what it is to be human, whether male or female. She tells my story, and that of many of my clients through the years, with poetic grace and a love of life so profound it will break your heart open if you let it.

My invitation to you is this: curl up in your favorite reading place with a cup of tea, take a sweet relaxing breath, then read these words aloud as a gift to yourself. Let them deepen your self-love, inspire your creativity, clear out old pain and finally, wrap you in the healing power of compassion. You, and I, and the whole world, truly deserve it.

Rev. Louisa A. Dyer, MA
Spiritual Life Coach, Author, Radio Host
www.louisadyer.com

Introduction

As women, we have a special story to tell. It is a story that binds us together through our inherent nature as Life Givers, Lovers and Nurturers.

Like our Great Mother Earth, we have the innate pull to create and re-create, give birth and make anew what needs to be re-born from the ashes of pain or destruction. Everything we generate in this world in all areas of our lives flows from this place of knowing that our essential tendency is to love, protect, nurture and give of ourselves for the sake of others, for the sake of life itself. Yet, as women, we are vulnerable in our sharing of ourselves, often not appreciated for who we are. The danger is that when we can't be real, others cannot mirror themselves in our strength.

This story poem lived inside of me for a long time. It must have been brewing and growing with each event and experience that left its imprint on my life. In the process, I have realized that we are not bound by others' truth. We can and must re-write our story in order to awaken, to unbury our true selves and honor our unique truth. I share mine with you here, and assure you that yours lives within you.

Our story lives not in the messiness of events or people who love or hurt us, but in the meaning we give to those encounters. Let us take steps to reconnect our inner and outer worlds, to re-write the script of our story and give choice-full meaning to our lives so they align with our purpose and calling.

Discovering only in 2011 that I can write in this way, I am honored to share "Archaeology for the Woman's Soul" with you. This story-poem poured out of me, completing itself in about three weeks. This poem chose me and I feel deeply humbled to honor you through it.

I have learned that expressing myself in poetry, unbound by definitions, grammatical rules, punctuation or stanzas, can be incredibly liberating, inviting you now to became familiar with this process for your own healing and growth. It is only a matter of how much permission you give yourself to fall to your knees in awe at the marvel of what life brought for you. No censoring, no borders, no beginning and no end, no limit to what is possible. It is a matter of surrendering to what is, with a sense of gratitude for what once was and now is only a distant memory that no longer defines you, instead tells the story of what you are made of .

"Archaeology for the Woman's Soul" was born in the aftermath of claiming my freedom once more in my life. But something was different now. There was no anger left in me, no judgment, no regrets. Claiming my freedom this time was an act of pure self-love, not because I loved less, but because I finally learned to love myself more.

So walk this journey with me for a moment; reflect on your own experience until you unearth the profound wisdom that dwells in you. Claim it, and your own place in the world, using your True Voice to be clearly heard by all those who can benefit from it. Awaken Woman...Unearth Yourself...Worship Your Truth. Let your Light shine bright and the world will be a better place for all of us.

Unearth Yourself,
Corina Luna Dea

Contents

Prelude

Oh! Woman...
When the day breaks free
When the night unfolds
When naked you stand in front of the world,
Within the silence of your eyes
What passion stirs your magnificent heart?
What story wants to unfold
What lovers from the past come to your mind
What dreams want to have
A real and meaningful life?

Perhaps you want to know
Who am I now?
Who have I become
What forces made me who I am
Wondering,
How can I change if I choose so?
Your story, your pain, your hopes,
Your voice...
All concealed they are deep within the void
Hidden from your sight
Waiting for your heart
To split wide open
And journey far beyond
To an enchanting land
Imbued with your dreams and visions,
The place in your heart

2

Where all becomes real
Where all dimensions collide...
Where time and space no longer make sense
The world you can't see with your eyes
Suddenly becoming deeply profound...
Your eternal Soul fully embracing
The challenges you came on this Earth
To learn from and overcome.

So, let us take this journey together
To the depth of your Being
Awaken, Woman
Worship your Truth...
Unleash your Voice...
Open your Consciousness...
Dream your Dreams
Envision the world you want to create
'Cause nothing stands in your way
Once your mind and heart
Become intertwined.
Your power is beyond measure
You just have to believe
That everything you need
Is already within...
Manifesting all
Your passions and yearnings,
Longings and wildest desires.

So, now...
Take out the map to your Soul
Created so long ago,
Before you were born
And journey to your heart...
Allow the moon to shine upon your mind
Allow the stars to guide you in the night
Allow the trees to shade you
When tired you become!
You are never alone,
And never will you be
I promise you that...
Your Soul, your angels, your Higher Self
Have been on standby
For a long long time...
Waiting for your awakening
For your conscious self
To be alive and ready to dwell
In the sacredness of life
Reserved all for you
From the dawn of time.

Oh, Woman...
Embrace your inner Goddess,
Worship your own Truth
Unleash your Voice
Heal the centuries old wound

4

Forgiving all,
Even the unforgivable...
Accepting all
Blaming no more,
For in the long run
It does not matter at all
Why or how
Unconsciously you consented
To give your power away
To patriarchs...
To those you believed
To be stronger than you.

For now the time has come
To speak your truth
To stand in your power
Surrendering once and for all
To your highest calling and inner desire,
To shine your bright light
To blossom like a flower
Complete and whole
In flow with your Passion for Life
Claiming once and for all
Your place in the Universal Puzzle
As Mother, Healer and Lover...

The Descent

My dear friend,
I know what it takes to manifest
As well as what stands in the way,
I know your sorrow
I know your tears...
For on the same land
Together we have fought
For our worth,
For knowing that we matter
For being seen,
Accepted and once again valued...

You looked without,
You looked at the heavens
You went to the temple, you went to church
You went to school, you started a business
And yes, accomplishment is sweet
That book you have written
The gazing at the stars
The smile of your first child
All worthy of bowing to the ground...
With all these being said,
Why do you still feel empty?
What is the price to pay for meaning?
What can you do to know
Deep in your heart without a single doubt
That you matter, are enough, fulfilled
And truly significant!

Yet all you seek is not without...
Freedom
Peace
Love
Self-confidence
and...
Self-esteem...
Treasures kept hidden
Beneath the shell of life,
Beneath layers of love,
Beneath the crust of pain...

Looking within,
Acquiescence to answers come
Judge you do not...
Just sit and see
What truth breaks out
And kindly ask...

What story dwells within my breath?
What pains my bones endured?
What is my flesh reflecting from within,
When staring in silence from a distance...
When words are emptied
Of their own existence?

Your life broken in pictures made perfect,
Still fragments of your being

Glimpsing in your eyes.
A memory of anger crossing your spine
Remembering the smell of grass
The smell of sweat you so despise...
A dress you couldn't have as a child
A doll that money could not buy
A poem you could not write
A word you were afraid to speak out...

Behold! You are in the present now
Your body
Still speaks of memories you stored
Deep within your cells,
Deep within your mind
Trapped in the corners of your heart...
Your voice still a whisper
Your hands still feeling unsure
Your truth still hidden...
Waiting to be revealed
And made real...
Once and for all
Crossing over to the other side of fear...

And so, tired of it all...
You said: ENOUGH!
Deciding to dig,
Dig deep at the core of your being

Your story calling you out from within...
It wants to be alive!
To connect with the present
To connect with the past...
To dream of the future
Yet to become manifest.

Your shadow begins dancing with your Self
Don't push it away
It is a friend,
It's not the enemy
Never too far, never too close
Narrator and narrative
Wrapped in one presence
Exquisite embodiment of myth and truth

Your past flowing slowly into the present
Unveiled by the need to become
What you were always meant to be...
Embracing yourself without restraint
A Woman of women
A Goddess of beauty
A Pillar of strength,
Shaping your own path
Bringing together
With the love of your heart
Scattered pieces of your incredible life.

But wait...
Don't pick them up while still breaking
Let them all fall to the ground...
Let them settle,
Let them become acquainted
With each other,
Let them twist and turn
While taking the time to watch
The magic of the hour glass
Doing its own healing
Using its own wisdom
Re-inventing the future,
Emerging with the path
Already created by the Universe,
Long before your time on Earth
When still wrapped in the womb
Of a primordial existence,
Longing for air to breathe
Wanting to be free
With the same craving
The earth meets the rain
When thirsty for love
When hungry for becoming...

Majestic sister,
You will feel it deep in your core
When ready you are

To make sense of the mess
To make sense of the chaos
Seeking wholeness
Through metamorphosis,
Like a butterfly,
Growing your wings,
Ready to fly
Sharing your Essence,
Healing the world over
With your feminine fragrance.

Oh, Awaken Woman
Unearth Yourself
Worship your Truth
Unleash your Voice
Begin the excavation
Decide to soil your hands
With pieces of your life
Scattered on the ground
You left unharmed...
Awaiting for your labor of love
For self, for the girl inside of you
For the mother still weeping
For the grandmother still hoping
For Mother Earth still hurting...

Heal your wounds, oh beautiful woman...
Set us all free...

For as you heal,
The whole world heals with you!
You know your story
Your body speaks of it
You know it by sound
You know it by feeling
You know it by smell
You know it by touch
You know it by taste
When you swallowed the cup given to you,
When you touched the edge of endurance
When your eyes reflected the shame,
When you said "Yes"
When you said "No"
When your heart was not in it,
Yet you went along
For duty's sake, for children's sake,
For love's sake, for God's sake...
While every cell in your body
Was screaming
What are you doing?
Have you lost your mind?

And crazy you were not,
But drunken with loyalty
To what truth should be
Be normal, you were told,
Be a good girl,

Be sweet, be kind
Don't stand out too much
Stay in the back of the room
Sit in the back of the bus
Don't make waves
Be humble and proper
Learn how to cook and clean
How to pray and how to praise!

And so you did, and so did I
Women with a powerful voice
Forced to deny
Forced to be unseen
Forced into hiding
Preparing our hearts to give,
Never to receive!

We never learned how to ask
We never learned how to be
Dreamers without the ability to dream
Denying our Divine Being
Who am I to ask?
What good have I done to receive?
So let me please others some more
So let me buy the love,
Let me be worthy of good
For I have to earn a kind word,

A friendly smile
Oh! Let me please you, I said
Trembling within
My worth and self-esteem
Crashing to the dark ground
Under the burden of self-loathing,
Self-pity, while lacking forgiveness
For the self and others who so hurt me.
We allowed men to settle in our womb
Extracting the ambrosia and nectar
So needed by them
And we gave and gave some more
Until there was no more
Until we laid there empty,
Used, undeserving
Soiled by unfulfilled desires
Our bodies remembering what love should be
Yearning for flames of love
And passionate fires!

So...Awaken Woman!
Stand up!
Stand tall!
Stand apart!
Fall in love with your own self
Fall in love with who you are
Fall in love with life.
Fall in love with the pain...

Embracing it all as total perfection
Before you open your heart to the world!

Treasure yourself
Dig deep within your Soul
Excavate your past, the present...
The distant future
Bring out the gems and let them shine.
Unearth with your bare hands
The continuum of past lives
Of lovers you enchanted
Of kings you entertained,
The fields you plowed with your sweat
The silk that draped around your waist
Unfold it now on the ground

Unearth yourself,
Dig deep within your Soul
Wrap your magical hands
Around the wounds still hurting
For once you do,
Your heart will be free
And ready to love again,
From a healthier place within
Abundant with grace
Full of gratitude,
Forgiveness for self and others
Peace of mind and so much desire.

Honor your voice of truth,
No longer sitting on the fence
Now sharing freely from your Soul
What life has taught you
While getting your hands dirty
Cleansing you past
Of what could stand in the way
From living true
To who you are becoming

Free yourself, sweet sister
For there is nothing to regret,
Nothing to hold on to,
Nothing to still cry about!
Your past is not who you are,
You are what you're becoming!

Loving what is, is not an easy task,
I know...
Yet is the only way!
Surrender to what is
Without wanting to change it
Allow it to unfold,
Stand back and watch
Detached from the outcome
Observe...
And maybe that's enough!

Beloved sister...
Always choose the path of least resistance!
What explanation do you want?
What can they tell you?
What do you need to hear to be free?
I am so sorry...please forgive me...
I was wrong
Your mother giving back
The years of your childhood
Your father admiring your strength
Your teacher praising you in school
Your friend returning the boy she took
Your lover begging on his knees,
The looks he gave to other women...
Erased from the past
As if they never occurred.
Would that be enough?
What do you need in order to feel free,
While shouting to the whole world
That you are no longer
A victim of your circumstance?

My Story

I am not sure when I became a woman
The line became blurred
When innocence was lost
Translating what unfolded
To what should have never been
Before time, age lost its meaning
Too soon...too fast...
Life passed me by in adulthood,
Without a container
To capture the moments.
Precious they must have been
But, I wouldn't know!
Lost forever are the memories
I could not bear
I don't know in what part of my heart
Still they are hiding,
For now my eyes seek like a hawk
That which was lost
Now I am ready,
I need to bring them back!

Now, I am ready to re-enter my story,
Sift through the forgotten past
Lost pieces, lost memories
Still buried deep within
Awaiting for my love
So much of it I have right now,
Abundance fills my Soul

The silence was broken
Shattered to the ground
When time was right
When no more I could endure
Living on the edge of discomfort!

Forced to stand at crossroads often
Thoughts descend slowly in my heart
Opened only by a raging fire
Burning the grass caressing my feet
The neighbor took what was not his
When too young to cry out
For no one would listen in the dark!

The stitches I wear on my left arm
Speak of that day...
A lost soul pursuing salvation
Through anger!
I felt my pain and his
Seeking a place of its own
For broken we both were...
Orphaned in a world without mercy
Asking for what mortals define as truth
Detached from the earth,
But seeking its wonders
Abused and abuser swaying in the moment
A macabre dance of give and take
Feeding on each other without a knowing

Of what is truly about to happen.

Oh, well...in retrospect I know it all...
What did I do wrong?
I just went to get bread
And the heavens let loose...
Over bread?
Over a glass of water?
Over a spoken word?
Often he reached for my neck,
He must have liked my jewels
His hands coming together in prayer
Wrapped in naked eyes
Controlling the moment
With violent despair
Obsessive need to be a man
Hopelessly running from a deeper truth
About his own long forgotten pain,
Wondering in what way
I was triggering his anger...

That chapter of my life is long closed
Now I see glimpses of it
Through a fog of memories
No longer speaking of that day,
But the time that came about
Bringing along
So much change

So much transformation
So much beauty
So much compassion
So much understanding
Now feeling what life is all about,
Uprooting my thoughts
From a muddy existence
Freeing myself from the shackles
Of someone else's way of life
Into fully embracing my own.

Now...
Without reservation, without shame
Without fear of being exposed
I walk in the night
As in the brightest day light
Now my Soul soars to the skies
Singing in joy the song of freedom
Of peace of mind
Content...without any regret...
Even though it was not always so...

Oh, how precious my life is now
And ready I was at one time
To throw it all away
To take it away
As if it meant nothing
As if it were empty and without value.

I have asked for forgiveness
For so wrong I was
To diminish my Soul, my existence
The gift of life
So precious
So rare
So worthy of love
Of enjoyment and happiness
Total ecstasy,
And everlasting delight!

What would anger mother?
Oh, how I wanted to please her
To no avail was my attempt
Her own demons
Expressed the hate she had for self
What could I have done?
My world too small to know the truth
My eyes too blinded by the force of duty
My heart too heavy
With the pain of past lives
For none of us come in this world
A free Being....
My Gypsy ancestors
Screamed from the past
Their pain flew into my present
Overwhelming my senses
With their loud cries

Enslaved by the strong,
Giving my power away,
Continuing the legacy for years to come
Forty I might say...
A long time to be in the dark
Knowing nothing of what it could be
Broken by life, fragmented by echoes
Raptured in agony
And flattened to the ground.

And mother was angry,
Bitter, sick and loving!
Confusing me so
About what love is meant to be,
I can't speak! I can't cry!
I can't love! I can't die!
I said, when journeyed alone
Through the dark night of my Soul.

In school...the Communist terror...
Labels they used...a traitor I was...
Mentally challenged and poor in math
Couldn't sing right
Couldn't play ball right
Couldn't remember right
Couldn't draw right
What am I good at, I was thinking?
Nothing! I then concluded...

And years passed by
And older I became
Still thinking "nothing" of myself...
But one day stands out!
I spoke up against the institution
When just sixteen years of age
Injustice made my blood boil
Rushing to my head
My stomach turning upside down
And inside out...
While slamming the old heavy door
With strong ancient hinges!
I used profanities and bad names
Against the status quo...
So off I was sent, never to set foot
In that establishment again.
My high school years,
My education was stunted
And labor did I start
It broke my back, it broke my spirit
In fact, my soul was already gone
Some years ago
When I had to hide,
When blood came out of my flesh
When mother was mad
At my falsifying a score
In the fourth grade.

Unloved I felt
Unwanted and discarded
Like a bag of bones
Left in an ancient cave,
Perhaps I was digging my own grave
For wanting so much
For begging so deeply
For pleasing without restraint
For wanting to be loved
With all my imperfections.

My needs left untouched...in time...
Resentment set in...
Anger and sorrow
Emanating through my skin
Attracting more
Of what I was feeling within,
Unworthy of life
Unworthy of being
Attached to the outcome
Detached from myself
A people-pleaser I became.

I gave and gave and gave some more
The seed of my giving
Falling on barren ground
The wind came about
And blew it all away

The rain washed it off
With each heavenly drop.

In retrospect,
I learned that...
Nothing was wrong with my giving
But the place within my heart
The intention behind my actions
Was not made of soul stuff
It was the Ego, not my healthy Self,
Doing the loving, doing the giving
It was the need to be loved
The need to feel worthy through "Doing"
For my "Being" was not yet
Claimed from the past.

In my righteousness I was the victim
The whole world was against me
And the walls went up!
I built them so well
That no one could climb
To mend my broken heart...
I went into hiding
And stayed there for a very long time.

To function somewhat normal
I borrowed masks
All sorts of masks...

Some were pretty, some hideous,
Some went unnoticed in the dark
I was ashamed, I was dishonest
I cheated in school, in life
Unveiled were my games
Oh! The games people play...
I was a good player trying to fit in
Doing what's right, hiding the wrong
Avoiding judgment, running from truth
What truth? I had no truth.
All was a lie...
For who am I?
This is the question
That shook me up one day...
I felt naked and exposed
Wanting to hide some more
The shame of my emptiness
Was too much to withstand
Shattered to my very core
I began the digging at my holy site...

With compassion, I looked around
Finding the ruins of my life
To the north was my dignity
To the south was my worth
To the east was my strength
To the west my compassion!
All there!

Nothing was lost
Just buried deep
Under layers of hope
And unfulfilled dreams...

The descent was long and arduous...
Painful to the bone...
Unfair to the journey of my Soul...
It crippled my senses,
My way of knowing right from wrong
For love was always an amalgam of both
Just as mother taught me
Through her own unresolved pain,
Abuse mixed with love...

Until one day I said: Enough!
I need to know right now
How do I rise above the sky?
I want to see the mountain top
Take me there,
I screamed in my despair
And my Soul showed up...

Woke me up from the hypnotic trance
Picked up the pieces of my heart
And showed me the way
To my resilience
My love, my pride, my honor

And all that was still
Pure and untouched
By bitterness and guilt and shame
And so much lack of trust
In what it means to be human
What it means to be kind and loving
Fully present with myself and others.

The Awakening

It's been a while since time stood still
The question still ringing in my mind
"Who am I?" I asked...
Divorced twice...I'm not a mother...
My home is gone, I hate my work...
My mind, my body, my soul
Resisting to know
The direction in which I should truly go.

And then it came...
A vision like no other before
Transformed forever,
The path unfolding itself
In all splendor
My body became the trunk of a tree
Strong, impressive, imposing
All of a sudden
My arms turned
Into branches
My fingers into twigs
As I grew deep roots within the Earth...

The Great Mother received me with love
My essence pushing deeper and deeper
Toward the core...
A warm feeling engulfing my heart
I felt safe and loved...and somehow...
In a split of a second

All my pain was gone!
She, the Great Mother swallowed it all
Unfettered my burdens...
My past, my present, my distant future
For none of it mattered anymore
As I became part of all that there is...
All that there was...
And all that shall be...
Timeless I became,
Unbound by a place
A feeling, an emotion or a thought...
And all of a sudden,
It happened that I was carrying
In my strong branches
The whole globe, the whole world.
Holding this beautiful sphere
My mind, my psyche,
My Soul became one
Dichotomies of good and bad,
Love and fear,
Day and night
All disappeared...into the ethers!

I bow to you,
Oh, Mother Earth
You placed yourself into my branches,
My arms caressed the pain you have endured
And then I knew

If you can do it, so can I!
I can love without resisting what is
I can stand awed by humanity
Raptured in the longing,
Yearning for a pure love
Accepting the day and the night
Surrendering to the moon in the dark
The sun that warms my flesh
The rain that washes off my pain.

I bow to you again,
Oh, Mother Earth
You showed me
My truth, my love,
My myth
You told me I'm perfect
In my imperfection!
You loved me as I am
And told me
I am not broken...
Fragmented...
Forgotten...
Unwanted...
Discarded...and
Insignificant!
You told me I matter!
You told me you need me
To heal the wars

The hunger
The cutting of your trees
The killing of your creatures
The polluting of your rivers
The blood shedding on your flesh.

You told me to hold you tight
And never let you go
For you yearn for me as much as I for you
For your peace
Your freedom
Your stirring of my Soul...
I held you tight that day
When you surrendered to me
And I to You...

In that magical moment
I met my mother crying all alone,
Along with souls
That pained me in the past...
I held them all in my heart,
My branches,
My canopy offered them shade
For so exhausted they were
Coming into this world
To inflict pain...
A gesture of self-sacrifice on their part
So I can see what I am made of,

How deep my compassion can be
How I can love unconditionally
No matter what
I had to endure.

Now I know,
It was revealed to me...
I can forgive myself and others
I can let go of blame,
Taking full responsibility
For the lessons I came here to learn,
For how I show up in the world
For how I allowed myself to feel small
For how I hurt others
While living my own truth.

Now awakened are all aspects of myself
No looking back
No turning back
For now I can no longer say
I didn't know any better!
The Great Mother revealed the way
To the unlimited potential
Resting within me
Showed me who I am
Accepting all
Becoming who I am
No longer hiding my Light

Now...
Ready I am
To let it all shine bright
Healing myself
And the Wound of the World.

The Ascent

Once you begin to seek within
Know that there is no turning back
To the reality you once believed in...
All your senses heightened they become,
You will see much deeper
You will love far longer
You will feel much stronger
You will hear sounds much softer.
The stones on your path
Will turn to petals of lotus
The clouds into angels
The grass into a comforting warm blanket.

You will speak the language of the trees
The birds, the jaguar
And the bees
Because...
You now feel free and complete!
Interdependent,
Interconnected,
Interbeing...
With all that's within and without
Friends with your inner Warrior...
Your Lover...
Your Mother...
Your Magician...and
Your Wise Fool

All sacred aspects of who you are
No longer denied, no longer disowned
Archetypes becoming your true Guides
Unearthed shadows from deep down under
Now, healthy and alive
Journeying along with you
Walking the path
To your own inner light.

But first, you must be willing
The journey to begin
The time is now,
You can no longer cry
For the past or for the present.
Be willing to open up
Like a serpent shed your old skin
Making room for the new YOU,
Renewing your vows to yourself,
Re-writing your story,
Letting go of the old myth
Re-claiming your place in the world
By giving a new meaning to your past
It will set you free...
To become all that you came here to be.

Be willing to eat
From the tree of knowledge

The contract your ancestors
Made in the Garden of Eden
Is not real...is just a myth...
Suffering is not your cross,
And naked you are not...
No longer walk around in shame
Your eyes wide open
Can see through deception,
Dogma the world set upon you,
Without your consent
Enslaving all who accept it as truth.

Free yourself right now,
Sister of my heart
And begin a new script
Nothing is written in stone...
All can be undone...
Your brain, your cells, your thoughts
All re-programmed they can be
It requires only willingness to begin
On your part.

Transformation, change from within
Is a natural process,
Organic in its nature
It can't be rushed, it can't be stopped
It flows when ready you decide to be

For you have the power
Always within your very being.

Free will is yours to have
Always has been
Always will be
Granted you seek
Your place in the world
Engaging and embodying
Your Authentic Self,
When you work, speak, sleep and walk
When you pray and meditate
When you give thanks
To the stars and the moon
Becoming ONE
With all that is sacred...
For nothing is profane,
Everything has meaning
According to the intention you set,
And the attention you willingly choose
To build your life upon!
A rock that sustains you
When life trembles under your feet
When you have no one to turn to.

For what is there, but pure love
When all is unveiled and revealed?

The cradle of life,
The cradle of fire
Passion
Creation
Forgiveness
Total integration
Into the whole of creation...
The Collective Mind,
Intelligence beyond measure...
A Sacred space we all belong to,
Contributing consciously or not
To the Greater Good
Of all humankind!

Beloved sister,
Surrendering to what is
May be harder than it seems,
Requiring trust,
Acceptance,
Compassion,
Allowing truth to surface
Without trying to fix it
Or even change it
Soon, coming to realize
That first we must feel lost
In order to be found...
To recreate the story of "I Am"
Releasing labels or names

Embracing infinite possibilities
Allowing heart and Soul
To receive
The abundance of love
Flowing unbound throughout the Universe.

For life is a true paradox
What seems right could be wrong
And what is good could still be harmful...
In the end proving
How lessons can be learned
In ways we don't always understand.
So let time pass...
Let time flow on its own
One day, in Divine timing
In retrospect you will know
What it all means...
Why did he leave?
Why did I stay?
Why did I hurt?
Why did I not die?

In silence and reverence,
I invite you to seek
Within the feeling, the emotion
That's still keeping you trapped
In loneliness and anger
Where in your body do you feel it?

Does it have a color?
A shape?
A texture?
A taste?
Slowly touch with your mind's eyes
That place within your heart
And ask:
Am I truly sure
This is the ultimate truth?
Perhaps if I look a little deeper
Another truth will rise!
Perhaps I'm not a victim
Perhaps I am not abandoned
Perhaps I am not discarded,
For always another perspective is offered
When digging deeper than the surface.
As once a wise man said,
The mirror becomes cleaner and cleaner
As we go deeper within
No reflection, no projection
Of our own wound on the other
For the truth is,
What we can't stand in others
Is just a part of us
We still can't own completely
In our own lives.
So know that when we judge and criticize
Love becomes illusive...

For the two can't live together
Within the spaces of our heart.
Indeed,
The ultimate goal is to achieve freedom
Peace of mind...
Happiness and unconditional love
For the Self and others...

Falling in love with our own Self
Is not what we've been taught
How can I be selfish, you might ask?
How can I love myself more
Than I love others?
Kant, the philosopher, said in his thesis,
His Categorical Imperative...
That nothing has worth and value
Unless it comes from duty and sacrifice.

Well, that was then...
The age of sacrifice has ended
A new era has arrived!
We are evolving as a Whole
As souls we want to be real and original
Without pretense and manipulation
Masks we've been carrying for so long
Are now falling to the ground
Authentic we become,
In touch with our true self

Embracing the darkness
And judging no more,
The self, the self of others
Knowing with every breath we take
We are never alone
But part of the Collective
Part of the Whole...

As we journey along,
Teachers show up on our path...
The mirrors they hold
Are not always so pleasant...
Yes, loving the Self is somewhat
A long process
When all we've been told is to sacrifice
Our love, our pleasure,
Our soul and our mind
For other people's pleasure and comfort.

Oh, Woman...
End the cycle right now
Come undone
Become free
For the sake of your daughter,
For the sake of your son
Show them the way to their own truth,
Embracing who you are
Choosing the way to heal your heart...

Letting your body speak to you
The language of love,
The language of truth...

When seeking even deeper
What symptoms do you experience,
In the wake of the night?
What hurts,
What screams,
What needs your attention?
What relationship is stagnant?
What job do you despise?

So, please ask this one question:
What would I choose right now
If I would truly love myself
With all that I've got
Deeply and completely?
Would I leave?
Would I stay?
Would I cry?
Would I hide?

Dream slowly into who you are becoming
Feeling centered,
Confident and free...
It is a sign of self-love
It is the essence of self-care

Your true Self emerging from within
Your potential from the future
Claiming all of yourself
Choosing to live according
To your own Truth.

For remember, all that we embrace
Comes from two powerful emotions:
Fear or Love...
Which one dwells in your heart
Which one guides your decisions
Which one do you dance with
In the silence of the night?
Fear not, no more of that
Your truth is yours to own!
Claim it now,
Wear it on your sleeves,
Paint it,
Sing it,
Speak it,
Write it,
Share it.
Convey it to the world
In any way you can and want!
But please, for God's sake
No longer hide...

Liberate your Essense
Worship your Truth,
Unleash your Voice,
Shout from the top of a mountain...
Your Message of Love
Your Sacred offer to the world.

Your freedom is in you,
Become it,
Live it...
No longer ask for permission,
To love,
To feel angry,
To speak up,
To forgive,
To let go,
To integrate
And...
To just be!

Remembering who you are
Is indeed the ultimate journey within
For just like the hero
In mythological stories
We must face our fears,
Demons and scary creatures

We must conquer fortresses and high towers,
Cross rivers and climb high mountains.
We must become friends with the wind,
Learn how to listen to the land,
Track mountain lions
And go with the flow.
For in the end, all we are doing
While trying to heal our pains and wounds
Is learning to undo
How others defined their own truth.
Imposed on us since we came on this earth!

The path of deconstruction
Of old antiquated beliefs
Requires time, patience and skill...
In the process, you might as well become
An Archaeologist of Your Own Soul
Digging deep within your core,
Searching and seeking
For your hidden talents and gifts.

Sift through the upper layers of dirt.
Soil your hands with pieces of the past
Unearth your hidden treasures,
Clean them up with love and compassion
And make them shine bright...
Become one with the flow of life
And never go against the grain again...

Grow roots and stand tall
Ascend with your feet on the Earth...
For grounded in the physical world
You must become
To feel the magic of the spiritual world.
For both are one
All is revered and sacred,
When growing from pure intention...
To live and love with all your might
To sing praises to all life unfolding
To treat the world
As the most precious jewel you discovered.

Remember the days when young you were
What called your interest?
What made you sing and play?
Talk to your inner child
Bring her back from the past
From a Higher Source within...
Bring back to life
All your desires, visions and missions
All your longings and passionate fires.

Perhaps you once loved to dance,
Perhaps you know how to draw,
How to count,
How to cook
Or how to sing!

Perhaps you can write
Perhaps you care so deeply
For all the whales,
The wolves and the owls...
Perhaps you love flowers and stones...
Perhaps you can climb mountains
Perhaps you can run
Perhaps you can build
Perhaps you can speak and motivate
Perhaps you can sit with the dying
Perhaps you can inspire and serve
From the goodness of your heart
Not because you are told so
Not because others want you to...
But because it's your Truth
Born to share in love
With the entire world!

Awaken Woman
Unearth Yourself
Worship your Truth
Unleash your Voice
Make magic
Make waves
Make love...
Create...
Whatever your precious heart desires!
For your own sake

For the sake of the world
In gratitude to Mother Earth...

For as you heal and love
From deep within your heart
The whole world vibrates
With passion, joy and bliss!
And then...
All is well
All is Whole
Within and without...

The time is NOW!
Awaken Woman
Unearth Yourself
Worship your Truth...
With reverence
Re-enter your Story
Excavate what matters...

Are you ready to share your Voice
With the whole world?